This book is for

_____

From:

_____

Date:

_____

CHRISTMAS ANGELS
Copyright © 2007 by Thomas Nelson, Inc.

Published in Nashville, Tennessee, by Thomas Nelson, Inc. in association with Lion Hudson plc.

Stories based on *The Holy Bible, International Children's Bible*®, copyright © 1986, 1988, 1999, 2005 by
Thomas Nelson, Inc.

Illustrator: Steve Smallman

Thomas Nelson® books may be purchased in bulk for educational, business, fundraising, or sales
promotional use. For information, please email SpecialMarkets@ThomasNelson.com.

Library of Congress Cataloging-in-Publication Data

Ellis, Gwen

Christmas angels / by Gwen Ellis ; illustrated by Steve Smallman.
   p. cm.
ISBN-13:978-1-4003-0854-5 (hardcover)
ISBN-10:1-4003-0854-2
1. Jesus Christ—Nativity—Juvenile literature. 2. Angels—Juvenile literature. I. Smallman, Steve. II. Title.
BT315.3.E45 2007
232.92—dc22

2007005581

Printed in China
07 08 09 10 11 KHL 5 4 3 2 1

Christmas Angels

READ AND SHARE™

Retold by Gwen Ellis

Illustrated by Steve Smallman

THOMAS NELSON
Since 1798

NASHVILLE   DALLAS   MEXICO CITY   RIO DE JANEIRO   BEIJING

Many years ago there lived a young woman named Mary. Soon she would marry Joseph the carpenter.

One day just before her wedding, Mary had a big surprise. The biggest surprise of her life!
A shining angel appeared . . . right in front of her!

The angel Gabriel said, "Don't be afraid. God is very happy with you. He has a special message for you." Mary was so afraid. But she didn't run away.

"You are going to have a baby," the angel told her. "You must name Him Jesus. He will be great, and He will be called 'God's Son.'" Wow! She was going to be the mother of the most important baby who ever came to earth.

When Joseph heard about the baby, he didn't understand. God loved Joseph. He wanted him to know what was going to happen.

So God sent another angel. The angel said, "Name the baby Jesus. Jesus means 'Savior', and Jesus will save people from sin." When Joseph heard God's plan, he got excited too.

One day Herod, the king of their land, made a new rule. He said all the people had to go to their family's hometown to be counted. Mary's and Joseph's hometown was far away. It was almost time for the baby to be born.

Joseph looked for a place to stay.
He finally found room for them
in a barn. Mary was so tired she
lay right down on the hay.

But off they went, *clippety-clop, clippety-clop* to Bethlehem town. When they got there, the little town was full of people. Mary was so tired. But where could she sleep?

And that's where God's baby Son was born— on the hay in a barn—and no one even paid any attention . . . at first.

Out on a hillside near Bethlehem, shepherds were taking care of their sheep. SUDDENLY the sky became so bright with light it hurt their eyes. They were frightened nearly to death.

"Don't be afraid," someone inside the light said. It was an angel with a new message. "I have good news for you. A tiny baby was born in Bethlehem town tonight. You will find Him sleeping in the hay."

Then the whole sky filled up with so many angels
no one could count them. They sang, "Glory to God!"
And then, just like that, the angels disappeared.

When the angels were gone, the shepherds hurried
to Bethlehem town as fast as they could run.
They found the baby in a barn,
sleeping in the hay.

The shepherds gave thanks to God. Then they tiptoed out of the barn. As soon as they were outside, they started talking to everyone they met about Baby Jesus.

King Herod was just about the meanest man in the world. When he heard about Baby Jesus, he didn't like it one bit. He didn't want the baby to grow up and become king and take away his throne. King Herod wanted to hurt the baby. But God was not going to let anybody hurt Baby Jesus.

God sent another angel to warn Joseph.
"Take the baby and Mary and go far away to Egypt,"
the angel said. "Stay there until I tell you it's safe
to come home." So Joseph got right up out of bed
and took Mary and Baby Jesus to Egypt.

After a long time, God sent one last angel to Joseph in a dream. "Get up and take the child and his mother and go home."

That awful old king was gone and could never hurt
them again. Mary and Joseph and little Jesus laughed
and sang as they went home to their own land.
God and His angels had kept them safe.

Today we don't see angels very often, but they are all around us. They watch over us and care for us when we sleep, when we play, when we are happy, and when we are sad. We don't get to see Jesus, either, but He is right next to us all the time. He is always taking care of us because He loves us the best of all.